The Little Book of Dandelions

Deborah Ashe

Copyright © 2022 Deborah Ashe

All rights reserved.

DEDICATION

To all the bees and some of the birds.

CONTENTS

	Acknowledgments	i
1	Dandelions	1
2	Foraging	Pg 12
3	Dandelion Coffee	Pg 18
4	Wine	Pg 23
5	Folklore	Pg 31

ACKNOWLEDGMENTS

I've been very lucky in that I have met a great many wonderful people over the years. This is for all of those that celebrate the Dandelion and give her space in their yard.

Dandelion

Taraxacum officinale.

DANDELIONS

Have you ever just looked at a Dandelion on a spring day and thought how beautiful it is? Behind that cheery yellow face and dramatically pointy leaves, lies a treasure trove of nutrition and medicine.

In this culture of glistening, pristine lawns and golf course worthy garden vistas, one might be forgiven for sighing when our friend Dandelion pops up her head. But all is not lost. There are many benefits to having her in your yard. Like your favourite aunt who always stays too long at Thanksgiving Dinner, we all love her but we are going to have a tough time getting her to leave. Here's an idea - just let her stay until she's done.

In spring, the first Dandelions in the garden are often the only food source for bees and other visiting pollinators and the longer grass and leaf piles house a myriad of slumbering insects. Just leave them alone until the ambient temperatures are consistently above 10 to 15 degrees Fahrenheit. The bees can feast to their heart's content and your grass will soon overshadow the Dandelions and crowd them out. Then you can mow as normal once they are gone.

Some folks prefer to mow them before they let their seeds fly, but I'm one of those people that can't get enough of them, so I let them self-

seed. Free food and medicine? Can't beat that. Did I mention a coffee substitute and wine too? Back to that later.

The common dandelion is a perennial, herbaceous (in other words; not "woody") plant that forms rosettes of leaves with yellow flower clusters rising from the center. Dandelions are found throughout all of the US and Canada, as they tolerate a wide range of conditions.

Despite the efforts of many to rid their lawns of them today, in the past the dandelion was held in much higher regard and recognized for its

medicinal, aesthetic, and nutritive benefits. Named for their "lion-toothed" leaves (*dent de lion* in French means 'lion's tooth'), a salad of dandelion leaves is packed with valuable vitamins and minerals.

Leaves and Flowers: Dandelions grow very close to the ground, with the rosettes of leaves growing directly from the top of the root. Dandelion flower heads, 1 to 2 inches in diameter, are composed of hundreds of individual ray-shaped flowers clustered together. Flowers grow on hollow stalks that can range from 2 to 24 inches tall. Fruit: Flowers develop into seed heads. Each seed is attached to a characteristic fuzzy structure called a 'pappus' that allows the seed to be carried by the wind. As a side note: these seeds are one of my favourite folklore mentions, with each 'pappus' carrying a wish for you.

The Science Bit

Family: Asteraceae (Compositae), *Taraxacum officinale*, Wiggers

Source: Simon, J.E., A.F. Chadwick and L.E. Craker. 1984. Herbs: An Indexed Bibliography. 1971-1980. The Scientific Literature on Selected Herbs, and Aromatic and Medicinal Plants of the Temperate Zone. Archon Books, 770 pp., Hamden, CT.

Common dandelion, *Taraxacum officinale* Wiggers, is believed to be native to Europe. Naturalized in many parts of the world, the plant is sometimes classified as *Leontodon taraxacum* L. and known as blowball, cankerwort, Irish daisy, priest's crown, swine's

snout, lion's tooth, puffball, white endive, or wild endive. A developing plant is characterized by a long, thick taproot, a rosette of short leaves, and a single hollow stem bearing a yellow flower, which turns into a round fluffy seed head at maturity. Upon injury, the plant exudes a milky latex or juice.

The reported life zone of dandelion is 5 to 26 degrees centigrade with an annual precipitation of 0.3 to 2.7 meters and a soil pH of 4.2 to 8.3

(4.1-31). The plant is a hardy perennial, adaptable to most soil conditions. Strong regenerative properties make it difficult to eradicate, and it is therefore a common weed in many locations.

Horticultural varieties of dandelion differing in morphological and chemical characteristics are available for cultivation.

Roots are generally harvested in spring or fall of the second year, while leaves and flower heads are gathered from cultivated and wild plants throughout the growing season.

The bitter plant resin found in both roots and above-ground parts contains taraxacin, taraxerin, taraxerol, taraxasterol, inulin, gluten, gum, potash, choline, levulin, and putin. The plant itself is nutritious, being high in vitamins A, C, and niacin.

Dried and ground roots are used for non-caffeinated, coffee-like beverages, as a flavoring agent in coffee and cocoa, and as an addition to salad dishes. Dandelion wine can be made from the leaves and flower heads. Young, tender leaves are used in salads and soups. Roots stored in fall may be stimulated under suitable environmental conditions to produce leaves for use in winter salads.

As a medicinal plant, dandelion has been considered to be an aperient, diuretic, stimulant, stomachic, tonic, and detoxicant. Dandelion tea has been used against fever, insomnia, jaundice, rheumatism, eczema and other skin diseases, and constipation. Common dandelion and other *Taraxacum* species have also been used against warts, cancers, and tumors. The dried root constitutes a crude drug, taraxacum, but appears to lack any real therapeutic value. Taraxacin in the plant resin may stimulate gastric secretions. Hypoglycemic effects have been noted in animals that are fed Dandelions.

Taraxacum kok-saghyz Rodin, or Russian dandelion, is from Turkestan and can be used for production of rubber (14.1-3). *Taraxacum mongolicum* Hand-Mazz. is employed in Chinese herbal medicine for detoxification, fevers, external wounds, congestion, stomach strengthening, and lactation stimulation. The resin of the plant contains taraxacin, taraxacerin, taraxasterol, taraxerol, pectinum, and choline.

Extracts of common dandelion and *Taraxacum laevigatum* D.C. are generally recognized as safe for human consumption.

THE LITTLE BOOK OF DANDELIONS

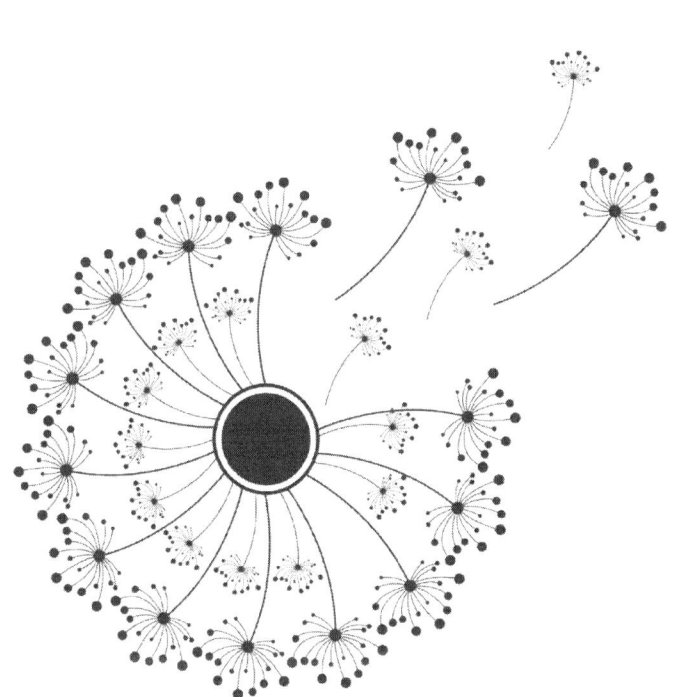

2 FORAGING

There is always value in knowing how to source food from places other than the local grocery store. Knowing how to use what the earth provides naturally could benefit us if ever an emergency arose. I always have mixed emotions about foraging, because if we all take the plants from the wild, there will be none left. Even taking a few leaves is fine for one person, but all of us? Nope.

I actually collect seeds and make my own personal 'foraging' patch in my garden. Not only am I in control of all the chemicals and conditions, but I am in control of how much is harvested. One Third rule. One for me, one for the birds and one for the plant.

Foraged edible plants like dandelions can dramatically increase your natural vitamin and

mineral intake, especially when they're growing in non-farmed soil which hasn't been depleted.

Always make sure to harvest dandelions from areas not treated with chemicals. This can complicate dandelion foraging as many lawns abundant with dandelions are also abundant with anti-dandelion chemicals. Don't forage on private property and be aware that the grass verges and walkways can have leached chemicals on them too. If your wild verge is near an immaculate lawn, chances are they have sprayed.

Dandelions can also have a positive impact on your grocery spending. While I'm not suggesting that foraging is the key to stretching your budget or to free food, it can absolutely be an effective layer – especially with a green as easily harvested as dandelions. Again, consider seeding your own spot, even a large container would do.

Dandelion has been used for centuries as a cleansing herb for ailments ranging from skin disorders, all the way to hepatitis. (I am not suggesting treating anything with dandelions, nor do I have the credentials to do so. I am only relaying past uses, and promoting dandelions as an excellent source of nutrition).

Dandelions are some of the most nutritious greens you can eat, boasting more antioxidants, vitamin C, A, and K than kale or spinach, and more calcium than milk! I personally think the green part of the plant is an excellent addition to my morning smoothie.

The young leaves are way less bitter than the older ones. You could even collect them and then blanch and freeze them to retain that flavour.

And, the entire plant is edible. Why not try your hand at frying dandelion blossoms. They are a unique tasting addition to your fritters. If you don't appreciate them solo, try adding a few to your other veggies, like potato or zucchini.

Choose bright, healthy-looking blooms to harvest. Try not to get any of the surrounding green parts as they are not tasty.

Dandelion petals are great for garnishing desserts, but one of the most common ways to prepare them is the aforementioned fried dandelion flowers, done by dipping in tempura batter and deep or shallow-fat frying.

3 DANDELION ROOT COFFEE

Like most herbals, dandelion root coffee can take a little time to get used to. We are so trained to like the mixtures that are available commercially, that it can be too 'earthy' at first. I suggest that you add things to it until you find a blend that you like.

Keep your main recipe separate and just add to each individual brew. That way you are not wasting any of your precious roots.

Don't forget that fine powders of all sorts are combustible. Protect yourself when grinding spices. No open flames and I do suggest either wearing a face mask of some kind, safety glasses if you have them or to mix things inside a large bag to stop the powders flying around all over your kitchen. Cinnamon powder in particular can easily irritate your nose and eyes.

Recipe 1.

Ingredients:

- 5 oz. dried dandelion root
- 5 oz. dried chicory root
- 5 oz. dried burdock root
- 1.5 oz. cacao nibs
- 1.5 oz. cinnamon

1. Measure ingredients.
2. Preheat the oven to 275 degrees Fahrenheit.
3. Spread the dandelion, chicory, and burdock roots onto a baking sheet. Roast the roots in the oven for approx. 2 hours, stirring every 20 minutes. Roots are adequately roasted when they are somewhat brown and have a toasty fragrance. Remove from the oven, and set aside to cool.

4. In a food processor, add the cooled roasted roots, cacao nibs, and cinnamon chips. Pulse until the mixture resembles the texture of coffee grounds, taking care not to produce too fine of a powder.
5. Transfer your ground herbal coffee blend to a jar with a tight-fitting lid and prepare as you would a regular pot of coffee. Use more of the blend if you prefer dark roasts, less if you lean toward lighter notes.
6. It's a good idea to label your jars with the date of roasting and to check it every now and again. If you feel that it is absorbing moisture you can pop it into the oven next time you are cooking, just to refresh that toastiness. If you have a dehydrator, of course you can use that, but I suggest slicing the roots into chips and laying flat on your dehydrator sheet.

Recipe 2.

This recipe makes a good dandelion Chai.

Experiment with spices that you like until you have a good blend. Make notes. Make them as you concoct your recipe because you will NOT remember them later. Label everything. Trust me.

Ingredients

- 4 cups water
- 2 tablespoons ground roasted dandelion root
- 2 tablespoons ground roasted chicory root
- 1 cinnamon stick

Instructions

1. Place water, dandelion root, chicory root, and cinnamon stick in a saucepan

2. Bring to a boil, then simmer for 5 minutes
3. Pour coffee into cups through a fine mesh strainer
4. Add coconut milk or heavy cream if desired
5. Serve

4 WINE

Recipe 1.

Ingredients

- 3 quarts dandelion petals
- 1 gallon water
- 2 oranges, with peel, preferably organic
- 1 lemon, with peel, preferably organic
- 3 pounds sugar
- 1 package wine yeast or champagne yeast
- 1 pound of raisins, preferably organic

Directions

1) Collect the blossoms when they are fully open on a sunny day. Remove any green parts. The green parts will really add bitterness to your concoction, so this is a very important step. Laborious and time consuming, but well worth it.

2) Bring the water to a boil and pour it over the flowers in a large pot or crock. Cover with a towel to keep dust out and let steep for three days. Stir daily to keep the petals submerged. They will develop a musty smell, which is normal.

3) Prepare the oranges and the lemon. Zest about half of the rind and peel off the rest in thin strips. You want to minimize the amount of

white pith added to the brew. Peel the pith off the fruit and slice into thin rounds.

4) Add the lemon and orange zest to the flower-water mixture and bring to a boil. Remove from heat, strain out solids. Dissolve the sugar in the flower water. Allow to cool to room temperature.

5) Add the yeast, orange and lemon slices, and raisins to the liquid. Put everything into a crock (or wide mouth carboy with airlock) to ferment. I cover my crock with a clean cotton towel held down by a rubber band to keep dust and bugs out. Stir daily with a wooden spoon or non-reactive stir stick.

Bottling the Wine

You have two options for bottling your homemade dandelion wine. You can let it finish in bottles, or move to a carboy and then bottle.

To finish in bottles: When the primary fermentation mixture stops bubbling (1-2 weeks), fermentation is almost done. Strain the liquid through several layers of cheesecloth or a flour sack towel and transfer to sterilized bottles.

Slip a deflated balloon over the top of each bottle to monitor for further fermentation. When the balloon remains deflated for 24 hours, fermentation is complete. I sometimes like to use fermentation locks for a while after that, just to let the last of the yeasts do their thing. They can fool you into thinking that their work is all done, and then a warm day comes along and they start again.

Cork the bottles and store in a cool, dark place for at least six months before drinking.

NOTE: Do not seal bottles tightly before they finish fermenting, and don't put them somewhere warm. That gas has to escape somewhere and if it means exploding bottles, it will certainly do that.

If you would like a clearer wine, rack the wine into a gallon carboy with airlock before the final bottling. Allow to ferment in the carboy for 2-3 months, and then rack into the bottles.

You could use finings and other wine making techniques here, but that's a personal choice. A lot of ingredients that are use for clarifying wines and brews are not suitable for vegans or vegetarians, so be sure to check. Not only for your own use, but if you serve to friends at a later date. You'll need to mark the bottles that are not vegan/veggie friendly.

Dandelion Mead Recipe

Ingredients

- 1 gal water
- 3 lbs honey
- 1 tsp Yeast Nutrient
- 1 g wine yeast
- 1 cup golden raisins (golden raisins will better keep the yellow color of the mead)
- 1.5 pints dandelion petals
- 1 Lemon

Directions

1. Collect 3 quarts of **Dandelion flower heads** in full bloom. Rinse any debris off the flower heads.
2. Separate the flower **petals** from the base of the blossoms. Remove as much green flower parts as possible from the petals. These add significant bitterness to the brew.

3. In a medium pot, boil 1 gal of **water**. Add one quart of the water to a mason jar with the petals, and put in the refrigerator and steep for 1 day.
4. Remove the rest of the water from heat, wait until the bubbles stop, add **honey**. Stir until the honey is fully dissolved.
5. Add this must, **raisins**, and **yeast nutrient** to a sanitized 2 gallon primary fermenter.
6. Seal fermenter with airlock and store for a day, until the must cools to about 70 degrees.
7. After a day of steeping, strain petals from the dandelion tea and add to fermenter.
8. Add the juice and zest of one **lemon.**
9. Aerate the liquid in the fermenter, and add the rehydrated **yeast**.
10. Put the fermenter in a dark place at a temperature of around 70 degrees.

11. After 2 weeks, with a siphon, re-rack the mead into a sanitized 1 gallon carboy.
12. After 4 weeks, re-rack, then let age for 6 months.
13. Fill sanitized bottles and let age for at least 5 more months.
14. Use as a spring celebration tonic.
15. Clean all your equipment and repeat. Make this a fabulous yearly tradition.

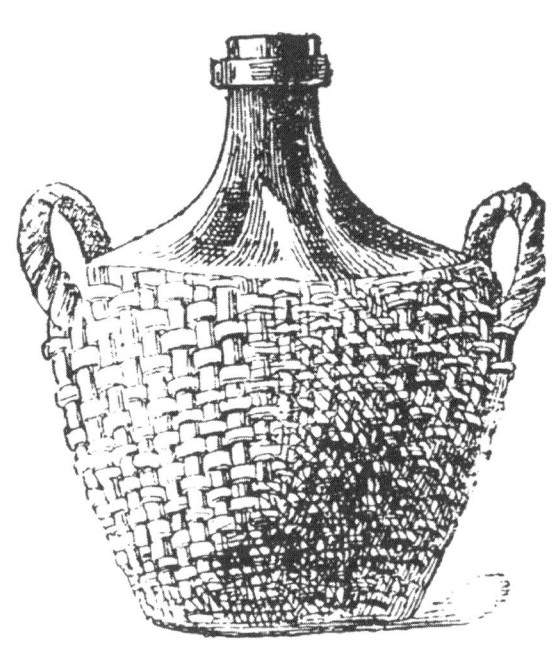

5 FOLKLORE

Dandelions have long been regarded as spiritual messengers, carrying messages from the divine realm to the earthly plane. Their delicate, ethereal appearance is believed to be a sign of their spiritual nature. Just as the wind carries their seeds far and wide, dandelions are thought to carry messages and guidance from the spiritual realm to those who are open to receiving them.

In many cultures, it is believed that when you make a wish and blow on a dandelion, the seeds disperse, carrying your wish to the universe. This act of blowing on a dandelion is seen as a form of communication with the spiritual realm, a way to send your intentions and desires out into the world. The dandelion's fluffy white seeds floating through the air are seen as a physical manifestation of your wishes being carried away and heard by the divine.

The dandelion's ability to grow and thrive in even the harshest conditions is seen as a symbol of resilience and the strength of the human spirit. Just as the dandelion can push through cracks in the pavement and bloom in unlikely places, it is believed that we too can overcome adversity and find beauty and growth in even the most challenging circumstances.

Dandelions as Symbols of Transformation

Dandelions are often associated with transformation and personal growth. Just as the dandelion transforms from a vibrant yellow flower to a delicate white puffball, it is seen as a symbol of the transformative power of change. The dandelion's journey from flower to seed represents the cycle of life, death, and rebirth.

In many spiritual traditions, the dandelion is seen as a reminder to embrace change and let

go of attachments. Just as the dandelion releases its seeds to the wind, we too are encouraged to release what no longer serves us and allow new opportunities and experiences to come into our lives. The dandelion teaches us to surrender to the flow of life and trust in the process of transformation.

Dandelions as Symbols of Wish Fulfillment

One of the most well-known symbolic meanings of dandelions is their association with wish fulfillment. The act of blowing on a dandelion and making a wish is a widespread belief that is deeply ingrained in many cultures. It is believed that when you make a wish and blow on a dandelion, the seeds disperse and carry your wish to the universe.

The dandelion's ability to grant wishes is seen as a manifestation of the power of intention and belief. By making a wish and blowing on a dandelion, you are actively participating in the co-creation of your reality. The dandelion reminds us that our thoughts and desires have the power to shape our lives, and by sending our wishes out into the world, we are aligning ourselves with the flow of abundance and manifestation.

THE DANDELION

With little teeth you hold the world entranced
Capturing the sun and glowing gold
Winter has left us needing rays of light
And this you provide with gusto to my delight
A snack for bees and children
A cure for many ills and woes
Your little yellow head just glows
With promise of a better day
You are an unsung hero of the modern world
Yet, you wait, your glory as yet unfurled.
Until the time is near for letting go
Until you rest once more under the snow.

Deborah Ashe

Printed in Dunstable, United Kingdom